W9-BQS-712

HERSHEY'S®

3 Books in 1

pil

Publications International, Ltd.

© **2011 Publications International, Ltd.**
Recipes and text © 2011 The Hershey Company.
Photographs copyright © 2011 Publications International, Ltd.
All rights reserved. This publication may not be reproduced or quoted in whole
or in part by any means whatsoever without written permission from:

Louis Weber, CEO
Publications International, Ltd.
7373 North Cicero Avenue
Lincolnwood, IL 60712

Permission is never granted for commercial purposes.

HERSHEY'S, HERSHEY'S Trade dress, KISSES, MINI KISSES, KISSES Conical
Configuration, HUGS, MAUNA LOA, HEATH, MOUNDS, REESE'S, SPECIAL
DARK and YORK are trademarks and trade dresses used under license from
The Hershey Company, Hershey, PA, 17033.

Pictured on the front cover (*top to bottom*): Mini Brownie Cups (*page 38*),
English Toffee Bars (*page 54*), and Mocha Brownie Nut Torte (*page 118*).

Pictured on the back cover (*top to bottom*): Rich Dark Tiger Cookies
(*page 84*) and Petit Mocha Cheesecakes (*page 98*).

ISBN-13: 978-1-4508-2359-3
ISBN-10: 1-4508-2359-9

Library of Congress Control Number: 2011921870

Manufactured in China.

8 7 6 5 4 3 2 1

Microwave Cooking: Microwave ovens vary in wattage. Use the cooking
times as guidelines and check for doneness before adding more time.

Sweet Treats

Contents

HERSHEY'S

Cookies

Fudgey Coconut Clusters

MAKES ABOUT 2½ DOZEN COOKIES

5⅓ cups MOUNDS Sweetened Coconut Flakes
1 can (14 ounces) sweetened condensed milk (not evaporated milk)
⅔ cup HERSHEY'S Cocoa
¼ cup (½ stick) butter or margarine, melted
2 teaspoons vanilla extract
1½ teaspoons almond extract
    HERSHEY'S MINI KISSESʙʀᴀɴᴅ Milk Chocolates or candied cherry halves (optional)

1. Heat oven to 350°F. Line cookie sheets with aluminum foil; generously grease foil with vegetable shortening.

2. Combine coconut, sweetened condensed milk, cocoa, melted butter, vanilla and almond extract in large bowl; mix well. Drop by rounded tablespoons onto prepared cookie sheets.

3. Bake 9 to 11 minutes or just until set; press 3 milk chocolates or candied cherry halves in center of each cookie, if desired. Immediately remove cookies to wire racks and cool completely.

Chocolate Chip Macaroons: Omit cocoa and melted butter; stir together other ingredients. Add 1 cup HERSHEY'S Mini Chips Semi-Sweet Chocolate. Bake 9 to 11 minutes or just until set. Immediately remove to wire racks and cool completely.

NEW CLASSICS AND OLD FAVORITES

Chewy Drizzled Cinnamon Chip Cookies

MAKES ABOUT 5 DOZEN COOKIES

¾ cup (1½ sticks) butter or margarine, softened

1 cup packed light brown sugar

¼ cup light corn syrup

1 egg

1⅔ cups (10-ounce package) HERSHEY'S Cinnamon Chips, divided

2½ cups all-purpose flour

2 teaspoons baking soda

¼ teaspoon salt

1 cup finely ground pecans or walnuts

CINNAMON CHIPS DRIZZLE (recipe follows)

1. Beat butter and brown sugar in large bowl until fluffy. Add corn syrup and egg; mix well.

2. Place 1 cup cinnamon chips in microwave-safe bowl. Microwave at MEDIUM (50%) 1 minute; stir. If necessary, microwave at MEDIUM an additional 15 seconds at a time, stirring after each heating, just until chips are melted when stirred. Stir melted chips into butter mixture.

3. Stir together flour, baking soda and salt; add to cinnamon chips mixture, beating just until blended. Cover; refrigerate dough about 1 hour or until firm enough to handle.

4. Heat oven to 350°F. Shape dough into 1-inch balls; roll in nuts, lightly pressing nuts into dough. Place on ungreased cookie sheet.

5. Bake 8 to 10 minutes or until golden around edges. Cool slightly; remove from cookie sheet to wire rack. Cool completely. Drizzle with CINNAMON CHIPS DRIZZLE.

Cinnamon Chips Drizzle: Place remaining ⅔ cup cinnamon chips and 1½ teaspoons shortening (do not use butter, margarine, spread or oil) in small microwave-safe bowl. Microwave at MEDIUM (50%) 1 minute; stir until chips are melted and mixture is smooth.

Peanut Butter and Milk Chocolate Chip Tassies

MAKES 3 DOZEN COOKIES

- ¾ cup (1½ sticks) butter, softened
- 1 package (3 ounces) cream cheese, softened
- 1½ cups all-purpose flour
- ¾ cup sugar, divided
- 1 egg, slightly beaten
- 2 tablespoons butter or margarine, melted
- ¼ teaspoon lemon juice
- ¼ teaspoon vanilla extract
- 1 cup HERSHEY'S Milk Chocolate Chips
- 1 cup REESE'S Peanut Butter Chips
- 2 teaspoons shortening (do not use butter, margarine, spread or oil)

1. Beat ¾ cup butter and cream cheese in medium bowl; add flour and ¼ cup sugar, beating until well blended. Cover; refrigerate about one hour or until dough is firm. Shape dough into 1-inch balls; press balls onto bottoms and up sides of about 36 small muffin cups (1¾ inches in diameter).

2. Heat oven to 350°F. Combine egg, remaining ½ cup sugar, melted butter, lemon juice and vanilla in small bowl; stir until smooth. Stir together milk chocolate chips and peanut butter chips. Set aside ⅓ cup chip mixture; add remaining chips to egg mixture. Evenly fill muffin cups with egg mixture.

3. Bake 20 to 25 minutes or until filling is set and lightly browned. Cool completely; remove from pan to wire rack.

4. Combine remaining ⅓ cup chip mixture and shortening in small microwave-safe bowl. Microwave at MEDIUM (50%) 30 seconds; stir. If necessary, microwave additional 10 seconds at a time, stirring after each heating, until chips are melted and mixture is smooth when stirred. Drizzle over tops of tassies.

Holiday Double Peanut Butter Fudge Cookies

MAKES ABOUT 3½ DOZEN COOKIES

1 can (14 ounces) sweetened condensed milk (not evaporated milk)
¾ cup REESE'S Creamy Peanut Butter
2 cups all-purpose biscuit baking mix
1 teaspoon vanilla extract
¾ cup REESE'S Peanut Butter Chips
¼ cup granulated sugar
½ teaspoon red colored sugar
½ teaspoon green colored sugar

1. Heat oven to 375°F.

2. Beat sweetened condensed milk and peanut butter in large bowl with electric mixer on medium speed until smooth. Beat in baking mix and vanilla; stir in peanut butter chips. Set aside.

3. Stir together granulated sugar and colored sugars in small bowl. Shape dough into 1-inch balls; roll in sugar. Place 2 inches apart on ungreased cookie sheet; flatten slightly with bottom of glass.

4. Bake 6 to 8 minutes or until very lightly browned (do not overbake). Cool slightly. Remove to wire rack and cool completely. Store in tightly covered container.

Oatmeal Butterscotch Cookies

MAKES ABOUT 4 DOZEN COOKIES

¾ cup (1½ sticks) butter or margarine, softened
¾ cup granulated sugar
¾ cup packed light brown sugar
2 eggs
1 teaspoon vanilla extract
1¼ cups all-purpose flour
1 teaspoon baking soda
½ teaspoon salt
½ teaspoon ground cinnamon
3 cups quick-cooking or regular rolled oats, uncooked
1¾ cups (11-ounce package) HERSHEY'S Butterscotch Chips

1. Heat oven to 375°F.

2. Beat butter, granulated sugar and brown sugar in large bowl with electric mixer on medium speed until well blended. Add eggs and vanilla; blend thoroughly. Stir together flour, baking soda, salt and cinnamon; gradually add to butter mixture, beating until well blended. Stir in oats and butterscotch chips; mix well. Drop by teaspoons onto ungreased cookie sheet.

3. Bake 8 to 10 minutes or until golden brown. Cool slightly on pan. Remove to wire rack and cool completely.

HERSHEY'S

BAKING &
Confection

KISSES Fluted Cups
with Peanut Butter Filling

MAKES ABOUT 2 DOZEN PIECES

72 HERSHEY'S KISSES_BRAND Milk Chocolates, divided
1 cup REESE'S Creamy Peanut Butter
1 cup powdered sugar
1 tablespoon butter or margarine, softened

1. Line 24 small muffin cups (1³/₄ inches in diameter) with small paper bake cups. Remove wrappers from chocolates.

2. Place 48 chocolates in small microwave-safe bowl. Microwave at MEDIUM (50%) 1 minute; stir. Microwave at MEDIUM an additional 10 seconds at a time, stirring after each heating, just until chocolate is melted when stirred. Using small brush, coat inside of paper cups with melted chocolate.

3. Refrigerate 20 minutes; reapply melted chocolate to any thin spots. Refrigerate until firm, preferably overnight. Gently peel paper from chocolate cups.

4. Beat peanut butter, powdered sugar and butter with electric mixer on medium speed in small bowl until smooth. Spoon into chocolate cups. Before serving, top each cup with a chocolate piece. Cover; store cups in refrigerator.

Secret KISSES Cookies

MAKES 3 DOZEN COOKIES

1   cup (2 sticks) butter or margarine, softened
1/2 cup granulated sugar
1   teaspoon vanilla extract
1 3/4 cups all-purpose flour
1   cup finely chopped walnuts or almonds
36   HERSHEY'S KISSES BRAND Milk Chocolates or HERSHEY'S
     KISSES BRAND Milk Chocolates with Almonds
     Powdered sugar

1. Beat butter, granulated sugar and vanilla with electric mixer on medium speed in large bowl until fluffy. Add flour and walnuts; beat on low speed of mixer until well blended. Cover; refrigerate 1 to 2 hours or until dough is firm enough to handle.

2. Remove wrappers from chocolates. Heat oven to 375°F. Using about 1 tablespoon dough for each cookie, shape dough around each chocolate; roll in hand to make ball. (Be sure to cover each chocolate piece completely.) Place on ungreased cookie sheet.

3. Bake 10 to 12 minutes or until cookies are set but not browned. Cool slightly; remove to wire rack. While still slightly warm, roll in powdered sugar. Cool completely. Store in tightly covered container. Roll again in powdered sugar just before serving.

Variation: Sift together 1 tablespoon HERSHEY'S Cocoa with 1/3 cup powdered sugar. Roll warm cookies in cocoa mixture.

KISSES Macaroon Cookies

MAKES ABOUT 4 DOZEN COOKIES

1/3 cup butter or margarine, softened
1 package (3 ounces) cream cheese, softened
3/4 cup sugar
1 egg yolk
2 teaspoons almond extract
2 teaspoons orange juice
1 1/4 cups all-purpose flour
2 teaspoons baking powder
1/4 teaspoon salt
5 cups MOUNDS Sweetened Coconut Flakes, divided
48 HERSHEY'S KISSES BRAND Milk Chocolates

1. Beat butter, cream cheese and sugar with electric mixer on medium speed in large bowl until well blended. Add egg yolk, almond extract and orange juice; beat well. Stir together flour, baking powder and salt; gradually add to butter mixture. Stir in 3 cups coconut. Cover; refrigerate 1 hour or until firm enough to handle. Meanwhile, remove wrappers from chocolates.

2. Heat oven to 350°F.

3. Shape dough into 1-inch balls; roll in remaining 2 cups coconut. Place on ungreased cookie sheet.

4. Bake 10 to 12 minutes or until lightly browned. Immediately press chocolate piece into center of each cookie. Cool 1 minute. Carefully remove to wire rack and cool completely.

Peanut Butter Blossoms

MAKES ABOUT 4 DOZEN COOKIES

48 HERSHEY'S KISSESBRAND Milk Chocolates
¾ cup REESE'S Creamy Peanut Butter
½ cup shortening
⅓ cup granulated sugar
⅓ cup packed light brown sugar
1 egg
2 tablespoons milk
1 teaspoon vanilla extract
1½ cups all-purpose flour
1 teaspoon baking soda
½ teaspoon salt
    Granulated sugar

1. Heat oven to 375°F. Remove wrappers from chocolates.

2. Beat peanut butter and shortening with electric mixer on medium speed in large bowl until well blended. Add ⅓ cup granulated sugar and brown sugar; beat until fluffy. Add egg, milk and vanilla; beat well. Stir together flour, baking soda and salt; gradually beat into peanut butter mixture.

3. Shape dough into 1-inch balls. Roll in additional granulated sugar; place on ungreased cookie sheet.

4. Bake 8 to 10 minutes or until lightly browned. Immediately press a chocolate into center of each cookie; cookies will crack around edges. Remove to wire racks and cool completely.

HERSHEY'S KISSES Birthday Cake

MAKES 10 TO 12 SERVINGS

2   cups sugar
1¾ cups all-purpose flour
¾   cup HERSHEY'S Cocoa or HERSHEY'S SPECIAL DARK
      Cocoa
1½ teaspoons baking powder
1½ teaspoons baking soda
1   teaspoon salt
2   eggs
1   cup milk
½   cup vegetable oil
2   teaspoons vanilla extract
1   cup boiling water
      VANILLA BUTTERCREAM FROSTING (recipe follows)
      HERSHEY'S KISSESBRAND Milk Chocolates

1. Heat oven to 350°F. Grease and flour two (9-inch) round baking pans or one (13×9×2-inch) baking pan.

2. Stir together sugar, flour, cocoa, baking powder, baking soda and salt in large bowl. Add eggs, milk, oil and vanilla; beat with electric mixer on medium speed for 2 minutes. Stir in boiling water (batter will be thin). Pour batter into prepared pans.

3. Bake 30 to 35 minutes for round pans, 35 to 40 minutes for rectangular pan or until wooden pick inserted in center comes out clean. Cool 10 minutes; turn out onto wire racks. Cool completely.

4. Frost with VANILLA BUTTERCREAM FROSTING. Remove wrappers from chocolates. Garnish top and sides of cake with chocolates.

VANILLA BUTTERCREAM FROSTING

MAKES ABOUT 2¹/₃ CUPS FROSTING

- ¹/₃ **cup butter or margarine, softened**
- 4 **cups powdered sugar, divided**
- 3 **to 4 tablespoons milk**
- 1½ **teaspoons vanilla extract**

Beat butter with electric mixer on medium speed in large bowl until creamy. With mixer running, gradually add about 2 cups powdered sugar, beating until well blended. Slowly beat in milk and vanilla. Gradually add remaining powdered sugar, beating until smooth. Add additional milk, if necessary, until frosting is desired consistency.

KISSES Christmas Candies

MAKES ABOUT 14 CANDIES

About 14 HERSHEY'S KISSES BRAND Milk Chocolates
3/4 cup ground almonds
1/3 cup powdered sugar
 1   tablespoon light corn syrup
1/2 teaspoon almond extract
     Few drops green food color
     Few drops red food color
     Granulated sugar

1. Remove wrappers from chocolates. Stir together ground almonds and powdered sugar in medium bowl until well blended. Stir together corn syrup and almond extract; stir or mix with hands until completely blended. Divide mixture in half, placing each half in separate bowls.

2. Add green food color to one part; with hands, mix until color is well blended and mixture clings together. Add red food color to other half; mix as directed.

3. Shape at least 1 teaspoon colored almond mixture around each chocolate. Roll in granulated sugar. Store in airtight container in cool, dry place.

CAKES &
Cheesecakes

Chocolate Syrup Swirl Cake

MAKES 20 SERVINGS

- 1 cup (2 sticks) butter or margarine, softened
- 2 cups sugar
- 2 teaspoons vanilla extract
- 3 eggs
- 2¾ cups all-purpose flour
- 1¼ teaspoons baking soda, divided
- ½ teaspoon salt
- 1 cup buttermilk or sour milk*
- 1 cup HERSHEY'S Syrup
- 1 cup MOUNDS Sweetened Coconut Flakes (optional)

To sour milk: Use 1 tablespoon white vinegar plus milk to equal 1 cup.

1. Heat oven to 350°F. Grease and flour a 12-cup fluted tube pan or 10-inch tube pan.

2. Beat butter, sugar and vanilla in large bowl until fluffy. Add eggs; beat well. Stir together flour, 1 teaspoon baking soda and salt; add alternately with buttermilk to butter mixture, beating until well blended.

3. Measure 2 cups batter in small bowl; stir in syrup and remaining ¼ teaspoon baking soda. Add coconut, if desired, to remaining vanilla batter; pour into prepared pan. Pour chocolate batter over vanilla batter in pan; do not mix.

4. Bake 60 to 70 minutes or until wooden pick inserted in center comes out clean. Cool 15 minutes; remove from pan to wire rack. Cool completely; glaze or frost as desired.

LUSCIOUS HOLIDAY DESSERTS

HERSHEY'S Chocolate Peppermint Roll

MAKES 10 TO 12 SERVINGS

CHOCOLATE SPONGE ROLL

4 eggs, separated
$\frac{1}{2}$ cup plus $\frac{1}{3}$ cup granulated sugar, divided
1 teaspoon vanilla extract
$\frac{1}{2}$ cup all-purpose flour
$\frac{1}{3}$ cup HERSHEY'S Cocoa
$\frac{1}{2}$ teaspoon baking powder
$\frac{1}{4}$ teaspoon baking soda
$\frac{1}{8}$ teaspoon salt
$\frac{1}{3}$ cup water

PEPPERMINT FILLING

1 cup ($\frac{1}{2}$ pint) whipping cream, cold
$\frac{1}{4}$ cup powdered sugar
$\frac{1}{4}$ cup finely crushed hard peppermint candy or $\frac{1}{2}$ teaspoon mint extract
Few drops red food color (optional)

CHOCOLATE GLAZE

2 tablespoons butter or margarine
2 tablespoons HERSHEY'S Cocoa
2 tablespoons water
1 cup powdered sugar
$\frac{1}{2}$ teaspoon vanilla extract

1. For CHOCOLATE SPONGE ROLL, heat oven to 375°F. Line $15\frac{1}{2}\times10\frac{1}{2}\times1$-inch jelly-roll pan with foil; generously grease foil.

2. Beat egg whites with electric mixer on high speed in large bowl until soft peaks form; gradually add $\frac{1}{2}$ cup granulated sugar, beating until stiff peaks form. Set aside.

3. Beat egg yolks and vanilla with electric mixer on medium speed in medium bowl 3 minutes. Gradually add remaining

$^1/_3$ cup granulated sugar; continue beating 2 minutes. Stir together flour, cocoa, baking powder, baking soda and salt. With mixer on low speed, add flour mixture to egg yolk mixture alternately with water, beating just until batter is smooth. Using rubber spatula, gradually fold beaten egg whites into chocolate mixture until well blended. Spread batter evenly in prepared pan.

4. Bake 12 to 15 minutes or until top springs back when touched lightly. Immediately loosen cake from edges of pan; invert onto clean towel sprinkled with powdered sugar. Carefully peel off foil. Immediately roll cake in towel, starting from narrow end; place on wire rack to cool completely.

5. For PEPPERMINT FILLING, beat whipping cream with electric mixer on medium speed in medium bowl until slightly thickened. Add $^1/_4$ cup powdered sugar and peppermint candy or mint extract and food color, if desired; beat cream until stiff peaks form.

6. For CHOCOLATE GLAZE, melt butter in small saucepan over very low heat; add cocoa and water, stirring until smooth and slightly thickened. Remove from heat and cool slightly. (Cool completely for thicker frosting.) Gradually beat in 1 cup powdered sugar and vanilla extract.

7. Carefully unroll cake; remove towel. Spread cake with PEPPERMINT FILLING; reroll cake. Glaze with CHOCOLATE GLAZE. Refrigerate until just before serving. Cover; refrigerate leftover dessert.

Variation: Substitute COFFEE FILLING for PEPPERMINT FILLING. Combine $1^1/_2$ cups cold milk and 2 teaspoons powdered instant coffee in medium bowl; let stand 5 minutes. Add 1 package (4-serving size) instant vanilla pudding. Beat with electric mixer on lowest speed about 2 minutes or until well blended. Use as directed above to fill CHOCOLATE SPONGE ROLL.

HERSHEY'S SPECIAL DARK Truffle Brownie Cheesecake

MAKES 10 TO 12 SERVINGS

BROWNIE LAYER

6	tablespoons melted butter or margarine
1¼	cups sugar
1	teaspoon vanilla extract
2	eggs
1	cup plus 2 tablespoons all-purpose flour
⅓	cup HERSHEY'S Cocoa
½	teaspoon baking powder
½	teaspoon salt

TRUFFLE CHEESECAKE LAYER

3	packages (8 ounces each) cream cheese, softened
¾	cup sugar
4	eggs
¼	cup heavy cream
2	teaspoons vanilla extract
¼	teaspoon salt
2	cups (12-ounce package) HERSHEY'S SPECIAL DARK Chocolate Chips, divided
½	teaspoon shortening (do not use butter, margarine, spread or oil)

1. Heat oven to 350°F. Grease 9-inch springform pan.

2. For BROWNIE LAYER, stir together melted butter, 1¼ cups sugar and 1 teaspoon vanilla. Add 2 eggs; stir until blended. Stir in flour, cocoa, baking powder and ½ teaspoon salt; blend well. Spread in prepared pan. Bake 25 to 30 minutes or until brownie layer pulls away from sides of pan.

3. Meanwhile for TRUFFLE CHEESECAKE LAYER, beat cream cheese and ¾ cup sugar with electric mixer on medium speed in large bowl until smooth. Gradually beat in 4 eggs, heavy cream, 2 teaspoons vanilla and ¼ teaspoon salt until well blended.

4. Set aside 2 tablespoons chocolate chips. Place remaining chips in large microwave-safe bowl. Microwave at MEDIUM (50%) 1½ minutes or until chips are melted and smooth when stirred. Gradually blend melted chocolate into cheesecake batter.

5. Remove BROWNIE LAYER from oven and immediately spoon cheesecake mixture over brownie. Return to oven; continue baking 45 to 50 minutes or until center is almost set. Remove from oven to wire rack. With knife, loosen cake from side of pan. Cool to room temperature. Remove side of pan.

6. Place remaining 2 tablespoons chocolate chips and shortening in small microwave-safe bowl. Microwave at MEDIUM 30 seconds or until chips are melted and mixture is smooth when stirred. Drizzle over top of cheesecake. Cover; refrigerate several hours until cold. Garnish as desired. Cover and refrigerate leftover cheesecake.

Cinnamon Chip Applesauce Coffee Cake

MAKES 12 TO 15 SERVINGS

1 cup (2 sticks) butter or margarine, softened
1 cup granulated sugar
2 eggs
$\frac{1}{2}$ teaspoon vanilla extract
$\frac{3}{4}$ cup applesauce
$2\frac{1}{2}$ cups all-purpose flour
1 teaspoon baking soda
$\frac{1}{2}$ teaspoon salt
$1\frac{2}{3}$ cups (10-ounce package) HERSHEY'S Cinnamon Chips
1 cup chopped pecans (optional)
$\frac{3}{4}$ cup powdered sugar
1 to 2 tablespoons warm water

1. Heat oven to 350°F. Lightly grease 13×9×2-inch baking pan.

2. Beat butter and granulated sugar with electric mixer on medium speed in large bowl until well blended. Beat in eggs and vanilla. Mix in applesauce. Stir together flour, baking soda and salt; gradually add to butter mixture, beating until well blended. Stir in cinnamon chips and pecans, if desired. Spread in prepared pan.

3. Bake 30 to 35 minutes or until wooden pick inserted in center comes out clean. Cool in pan on wire rack. Sprinkle cake with powdered sugar or stir together $\frac{3}{4}$ cup powdered sugar and warm water to make smooth glaze; drizzle over cake. Serve at room temperature or while still slightly warm.

Fluted Cake: Grease and flour 12-cup fluted tube pan. Prepare batter as directed; pour into prepared pan. Bake 45 to 50 minutes or until wooden pick inserted in thickest part comes out clean. Cool 15 minutes; invert onto wire rack. Cool completely.

Cupcakes: Line 24 baking cups ($2\frac{1}{2}$ inches in diameter) with paper baking liners. Prepare batter as directed; divide evenly into prepared cups. Bake 15 to 18 minutes or until wooden pick inserted in center comes out clean. Cool completely.

Chilled Raspberry Cheesecake

MAKES 10 TO 12 SERVINGS

1½ cups vanilla wafer crumbs (about 45 wafers, crushed)
⅓ cup HERSHEY'S Cocoa
⅓ cup powdered sugar
⅓ cup butter or margarine, melted
1 package (10 ounces) frozen raspberries (about 2½ cups), thawed
1 envelope unflavored gelatin
½ cup cold water
½ cup boiling water
2 packages (8 ounces each) cream cheese, softened
½ cup granulated sugar
1 teaspoon vanilla extract
3 tablespoons seedless red raspberry preserves
CHOCOLATE WHIPPED CREAM (recipe follows)

1. Heat oven to 350°F.

2. Stir together vanilla wafer crumbs, ⅓ cup cocoa and ⅓ cup powdered sugar in medium bowl; stir in melted butter. Press mixture onto bottom and 1½ inches up side of 9-inch springform pan. Bake 10 minutes; cool completely.

3. Purée and strain raspberries; set aside. Sprinkle gelatin over cold water in small bowl; let stand several minutes to soften. Add boiling water; stir until gelatin dissolves completely and mixture is clear. Beat cream cheese, granulated sugar and 1 teaspoon vanilla in large bowl until smooth. Gradually add raspberry purée and gelatin, mixing thoroughly; pour into prepared crust.

4. Refrigerate several hours or overnight. Loosen cake from side of pan with knife; remove side of pan. Stir raspberry preserves to soften; spread over cheesecake top. Garnish with CHOCOLATE WHIPPED CREAM. Cover; refrigerate leftovers.

Chocolate Whipped Cream: Stir together $1/2$ cup powdered sugar and $1/4$ cup HERSHEY'S Cocoa in medium bowl. Add 1 cup ($1/2$ pint) cold whipping cream and 1 teaspoon vanilla extract; beat until stiff.

Brownies
& BARS

Toffee-Topped Cheesecake Bars

MAKES ABOUT 36 BARS

1⅓ cups all-purpose flour
1 cup powdered sugar
⅓ cup HERSHEY'S Cocoa
¼ teaspoon baking soda
¾ cup (1½ sticks) butter or margarine, softened
1 package (8 ounces) cream cheese, softened
1 can (14 ounces) sweetened condensed milk (not evaporated milk)
2 eggs
1 teaspoon vanilla extract
1⅓ cups (8-ounce package) HEATH BITS 'O BRICKLE Toffee Bits, divided

1. Heat oven to 350°F.

2. Combine flour, powdered sugar, cocoa and baking soda in medium bowl; cut butter until mixture is crumbly. Press onto bottom of ungreased 13×9×2-inch baking pan. Bake 15 minutes.

3. Beat cream cheese until fluffy. Add sweetened condensed milk, eggs and vanilla; beat until smooth. Stir in ³/₄ cup toffee bits. Pour mixture over hot crust. Bake 20 to 25 minutes or until set and edges just begin to brown.

4. Remove from oven. Cool 15 minutes. Sprinkle remaining toffee bits evenly over top. Cool completely. Refrigerate several hours or until cold. Cover; store leftover bars in refrigerator.

SIMPLY SATISFYING SWEETS

Mini Brownie Cups

MAKES 24 SERVINGS

$\frac{1}{4}$ cup ($\frac{1}{2}$ stick) light margarine

2 egg whites

1 egg

$\frac{3}{4}$ cup sugar

$\frac{2}{3}$ cup all-purpose flour

$\frac{1}{3}$ cup HERSHEY'S Cocoa

$\frac{1}{2}$ teaspoon baking powder

$\frac{1}{4}$ teaspoon salt

MOCHA GLAZE (recipe follows)

1. Heat oven to 350°F. Line small muffin cups ($1\frac{3}{4}$ inches in diameter) with paper bake cups or spray with vegetable cooking spray.

2. Melt margarine in small saucepan over low heat; cool slightly. Beat egg whites and egg in small bowl with electric mixer on medium speed until foamy; gradually add sugar, beating until slightly thickened and light in color. Stir together flour, cocoa, baking powder and salt; gradually add to egg mixture, beating until blended. Gradually add melted margarine, beating just until blended. Fill muffin cups $\frac{2}{3}$ full with batter.

3. Bake 15 to 18 minutes or until wooden pick inserted in center comes out clean. Remove from pan to wire rack. Cool completely. Prepare MOCHA GLAZE; drizzle over tops of brownie cups. Let stand until glaze is set.

MOCHA GLAZE

- ¼ cup powdered sugar
- ¾ teaspoon HERSHEY'S Cocoa
- ¼ teaspoon powdered instant coffee
- 2 teaspoons hot water
- ¼ teaspoon vanilla extract

Stir together powdered sugar and cocoa in small bowl. Dissolve instant coffee in water; gradually add to sugar mixture, stirring until well blended. Stir in vanilla.

Chocolate Orange Cheesecake Bars

MAKES 24 BARS

1   cup all-purpose flour
$\frac{1}{2}$ cup packed light brown sugar
$\frac{1}{4}$ teaspoon ground cinnamon (optional)
$\frac{1}{3}$ cup shortening
$\frac{1}{2}$ cup chopped pecans
     CHOCOLATE ORANGE FILLING (recipe follows)
     Pecan halves (optional)

1. Heat oven to 350°F.

2. Stir together flour, brown sugar and cinnamon, if desired, in large bowl. Cut shortening into flour mixture with pastry blender or two knives until mixture resembles coarse crumbs. Stir in chopped pecans. Reserve $\frac{3}{4}$ cup flour mixture. Press remaining mixture firmly onto bottom of ungreased 9-inch square baking pan. Bake 10 minutes or until lightly browned.

3. Spread CHOCOLATE ORANGE FILLING over warm crust. Sprinkle with reserved flour mixture. Press pecan halves lightly onto top, if desired. Return to oven. Bake 25 to 30 minutes or until lightly browned. Cool; cut into bars. Cover; refrigerate leftover bars.

CHOCOLATE ORANGE FILLING

1   package (8 ounces) cream cheese, softened
$\frac{2}{3}$ cup granulated sugar
$\frac{1}{3}$ cup HERSHEY'S Cocoa
$\frac{1}{4}$ cup milk
1   egg
1   teaspoon vanilla extract
$\frac{1}{4}$ teaspoon freshly grated orange peel
     Pecan halves (optional)

Beat cream cheese and granulated sugar with electric mixer on medium speed in medium bowl until fluffy. Add cocoa, milk, egg, vanilla and orange peel; beat until smooth.

Peanut Butter Fudge Brownie Bars

MAKES 36 BARS

1 cup (2 sticks) butter or margarine, melted
1½ cups sugar
2 eggs
1 teaspoon vanilla extract
1¼ cups all-purpose flour
⅔ cup HERSHEY'S Cocoa
¼ cup milk
1¼ cups chopped pecans or walnuts, divided
½ cup (1 stick) butter or margarine
1⅔ cups (10-ounce package) REESE'S Peanut Butter Chips
1 can (14 ounces) sweetened condensed milk (not evaporated milk)
¼ cup HERSHEY'S SPECIAL DARK Chocolate Chips or HERSHEY'S Semi-Sweet Chocolate Chips

1. Heat oven to 350°F. Grease 13×9×2-inch baking pan.

2. Beat melted butter, sugar, eggs and vanilla in large bowl with electric mixer on medium speed until well blended. Add flour, cocoa and milk; beat until blended. Stir in 1 cup nuts. Spread in prepared pan.

3. Bake 25 to 30 minutes or just until edges begin to pull away from sides of pan. Cool completely in pan on wire rack.

4. Melt ½ cup butter and peanut butter chips in medium saucepan over low heat, stirring constantly. Add sweetened condensed milk, stirring until smooth; pour over baked layer.

5. Place chocolate chips in small microwave-safe bowl. Microwave at MEDIUM (50%) 45 seconds or just until chips are melted when stirred. Drizzle bars with melted chocolate; sprinkle with remaining ¼ cup nuts. Refrigerate 1 hour or until firm. Cut into bars. Cover; refrigerate leftover bars.

White Chip Lemon Streusel Bars

MAKES 36 BARS

1 can (14 ounces) sweetened condensed milk (not
   evaporated milk)

½ cup lemon juice

1 teaspoon freshly grated lemon peel

2 cups (12-ounce package) HERSHEY'S Premier White
   Chips, divided

⅔ cup butter or margarine, softened

1 cup packed light brown sugar

1½ cups all-purpose flour

1½ cups regular rolled or quick-cooking oats

¾ cup toasted pecan pieces*

1 teaspoon baking powder

½ teaspoon salt

1 egg

½ teaspoon shortening

*To toast pecans: Heat oven to 350°F. Spread pecans in thin layer in
shallow baking pan. Bake, stirring occasionally, 7 to 8 minutes or until
golden brown; cool.*

1. Heat oven to 350°F. Lightly grease 13×9×2-inch baking pan.
Combine sweetened condensed milk, lemon juice and lemon
peel in medium bowl; set aside. Measure out ¼ cup and ⅓ cup
white chips; set aside. Add remaining white chips to lemon
mixture.

2. Beat butter and brown sugar with electric mixer on medium
speed in large bowl until well blended. Stir together flour, oats,
pecans, baking powder and salt; add to butter mixture, blending
well. Set aside 1⅔ cups oats mixture. Add egg to remaining oats
mixture, blending until crumbly; press onto bottom of prepared
pan. Gently spoon lemon mixture on top, spreading evenly. Add
reserved ⅓ cup white chips to reserved oats mixture. Sprinkle
over lemon layer, pressing down lightly.

3. Bake 20 to 25 minutes or until lightly browned. Cool in pan on wire rack. Place remaining $1/4$ cup white chips and shortening in small microwave-safe bowl. Microwave at MEDIUM (50%) 30 seconds or until chips are melted and mixture is smooth when stirred. Drizzle over baked bars. Allow drizzle to set; cut into bars.

PIES & Desserts

Deep Dark Mousse

MAKES 4 TO 6 SERVINGS

¼ cup sugar
1 teaspoon unflavored gelatin
½ cup milk
1 cup HERSHEY'S SPECIAL DARK Chocolate Chips
2 teaspoons vanilla extract
1 cup (½ pint) cold whipping cream
Sweetened whipped cream (optional)

1. Stir together sugar and gelatin in small saucepan; stir in milk. Let stand 2 minutes to soften gelatin. Cook over medium heat, stirring constantly, until mixture just begins to boil.

2. Remove from heat. Immediately add chocolate chips; stir until melted. Stir in vanilla; cool to room temperature.

3. Beat whipping cream with electric mixer on high speed in large bowl until stiff peaks form. Add half of chocolate mixture and gently fold until nearly combined; add remaining chocolate mixture and fold just until blended. Spoon into serving dish or individual dishes. Refrigerate. Garnish with sweetened whipped cream, if desired, just before serving.

SPECIAL CELEBRATION TREATS

Classic Chocolate Cream Pie

MAKES 8 TO 10 SERVINGS

5   sections (½ ounce each) HERSHEY'S Unsweetened
    Chocolate Baking Bar, broken into pieces
3   cups milk, divided
1⅓ cups sugar
3   tablespoons all-purpose flour
3   tablespoons cornstarch
½   teaspoon salt
3   egg yolks
2   tablespoons butter or margarine
1½ teaspoons vanilla extract
1   baked (9-inch) pie crust, cooled, or 1 (9-inch) crumb
    crust
    Sweetened whipped cream (optional)

1. Combine chocolate and 2 cups milk in medium saucepan;
cook over medium heat, stirring constantly, just until mixture boils.
Remove from heat and set aside.

2. Stir together sugar, flour, cornstarch and salt in medium bowl.
Whisk remaining 1 cup milk into egg yolks in separate bowl; stir
into sugar mixture. Gradually add to chocolate mixture. Cook over
medium heat, whisking constantly, until mixture boils; boil and stir
1 minute. Remove from heat; stir in butter and vanilla.

3. Pour into prepared crust; press plastic wrap directly onto
surface. Cool; refrigerate until well chilled. Top with whipped
cream, if desired.

SPECIAL DARK Fudge Fondue

MAKES 1 1/2 CUPS

2 cups (12-ounce package) HERSHEY'S SPECIAL DARK Chocolate Chips

1/2 cup light cream

2 teaspoons vanilla extract

Assorted fondue dippers such as marshmallows, cherries, grapes, mandarin orange segments, pineapple chunks, strawberries, slices of other fresh fruits, small pieces of cake or small brownies

1. Place chocolate chips and light cream in medium microwave-safe bowl. Microwave at MEDIUM (50%) 1 minute or just until chips are melted and mixture is smooth when stirred. Stir in vanilla.

2. Pour into fondue pot or chafing dish; serve warm with fondue dippers. If mixture thickens, stir in additional light cream, 1 tablespoon at a time. Refrigerate leftover fondue.

Stovetop Directions: Combine chocolate chips and light cream in heavy medium saucepan. Cook over low heat, stirring constantly, until chips are melted and mixture is hot. Stir in vanilla and continue as in Step 2 above.

Chocolate Pecan Pie

MAKES 8 SERVINGS

1   cup sugar
⅓   cup HERSHEY'S Cocoa
3   eggs, lightly beaten
¾   cup light corn syrup
1   tablespoon butter or margarine, melted
1   teaspoon vanilla extract
1   cup pecan halves
1   unbaked (9-inch) pie crust
    Whipped topping (optional)

1. Heat oven to 350°F.

2. Stir together sugar and cocoa in medium bowl. Add eggs, corn syrup, butter and vanilla; stir until well blended. Stir in pecans. Pour into unbaked pie crust.

3. Bake 60 minutes or until set. Remove to wire rack and cool completely. Garnish with whipped topping, if desired.

HERSHEY'S®

DECADENT DELIGHTS

Contents

HERSHEY'S

Brownies

& Bars

English Toffee Bars

Makes about 36 bars

- 2 **cups all-purpose flour**
- 1 **cup packed light brown sugar**
- ½ **cup (1 stick) cold butter**
- 1 **cup pecan halves**
  TOFFEE TOPPING (recipe follows)
- 1 **cup HERSHEY'S Milk Chocolate Chips**

1. Heat oven to 350°F.

2. Combine flour and brown sugar in large bowl. With pastry blender or fork, cut in butter until fine crumbs form (a few large crumbs may remain). Press mixture onto bottom of ungreased 13×9×2-inch baking pan. Sprinkle pecans over crust. Prepare TOFFEE TOPPING; drizzle evenly over pecans and crust.

3. Bake 20 to 22 minutes or until topping is bubbly and golden; remove from oven. Immediately sprinkle milk chocolate chips evenly over top; press gently onto surface. Cool completely in pan on wire rack. Cut into bars.

TOFFEE TOPPING: Combine ⅔ cup butter and ⅓ cup packed light brown sugar in small saucepan; cook over medium heat, stirring constantly, until mixture comes to a boil. Continue boiling, stirring constantly, 30 seconds. Use immediately.

HERSHEY'S

Championship Chocolate Chip Bars

Makes about 36 bars

1½ cups all-purpose flour
½ cup packed light brown sugar
½ cup (1 stick) cold butter or margarine
2 cups (12-ounce package) HERSHEY'S SPECIAL DARK Chocolate Chips or HERSHEY'S Semi-Sweet Chocolate Chips, divided
1 can (14 ounces) sweetened condensed milk (not evaporated milk)
1 egg, slightly beaten
1 teaspoon vanilla extract
1 cup chopped nuts

1. Heat oven to 350°F.

2. Stir together flour and brown sugar in medium bowl; cut in cold butter until crumbly. Stir in ½ cup chocolate chips; press mixture onto bottom of ungreased 13×9×2-inch baking pan. Bake 15 minutes.

3. Combine sweetened condensed milk, egg and vanilla in large bowl. Stir in remaining 1½ cups chips and nuts. Spread over hot baked crust. Bake 25 minutes or until golden. Cool completely in pan on wire rack. Cut into bars.

HERSHEY'S

Chippy Chewy Bars

Makes about 48 bars

½ cup (1 stick) butter or margarine
1½ cups graham cracker crumbs
1⅔ cups (10-ounce package) REESE'S Peanut Butter Chips
1½ cups MOUNDS Sweetened Coconut Flakes
1 can (14 ounces) sweetened condensed milk (not evaporated milk)
½ cup HERSHEY'S SPECIAL DARK Chocolate Chips, HERSHEY'S Semi-Sweet Chocolate Chips or HERSHEY'S Mini Chips Semi-Sweet Chocolate
¾ teaspoon shortening (do not use butter, margarine, spread or oil)

1. Heat oven to 350°F. Place butter in 13×9×2-inch baking pan. Heat in oven until melted; remove pan from oven. Sprinkle graham cracker crumbs evenly over butter; press down with fork.

2. Sprinkle peanut butter chips over crumbs; sprinkle coconut over chips. Drizzle sweetened condensed milk evenly over top.

3. Bake 20 minutes or until lightly browned.

4. Place chocolate chips and shortening in small microwave-safe bowl. Microwave at MEDIUM (50%) 30 seconds; stir. If necessary, microwave at MEDIUM an additional 10 seconds at a time, stirring after each heating, just until chips are melted when stirred. Drizzle evenly over top of baked mixture. Cool completely. Cut into bars.

HERSHEY'S

Thick and Fudgey Brownies with HERSHEY'S MINI KISSES Milk Chocolates

Makes 24 brownies

2¼	cups all-purpose flour
⅔	cup HERSHEY'S Cocoa
1	teaspoon baking powder
1	teaspoon salt
¾	cup (1½ sticks) butter or margarine, melted
2½	cups sugar
2	teaspoons vanilla extract
4	eggs
1¾	cups (10-ounce package) HERSHEY'S MINI KISSESBRAND Milk Chocolates

1. Heat oven to 350°F (325°F for glass baking dish). Grease 13×9×2-inch baking pan.

2. Stir together flour, cocoa, baking powder and salt. With spoon or whisk, stir together butter, sugar and vanilla in large bowl. Add eggs; stir until well blended. Stir in flour mixture, blending well. Stir in chocolate pieces. Spread batter in prepared pan.

3. Bake 30 to 35 minutes or until brownies begin to pull away from sides of pan. Cool completely in pan on wire rack; cut into 2-inch squares.

HERSHEY'S

Marbled Cheesecake Bars

Makes 24 to 36 bars

CHOCOLATE CRUST (recipe follows)

3 **packages (8 ounces each) cream cheese, softened**

1 **can (14 ounces) sweetened condensed milk (not evaporated milk)**

3 **eggs**

2 **teaspoons vanilla extract**

4 **sections (½ ounce each) HERSHEY'S Unsweetened Chocolate Baking Bar, melted**

1. Prepare CHOCOLATE CRUST. Cool.

2. Beat cream cheese in large bowl until fluffy. Gradually add sweetened condensed milk, beating until smooth. Add eggs and vanilla; mix well.

3. Pour half of batter evenly over prepared crust. Stir melted chocolate into remaining batter; drop by teaspoons over vanilla batter. With metal spatula or knife, swirl gently through batter to marble.

4. Bake 45 to 50 minutes or until set. Cool in pan on wire rack. Refrigerate several hours until chilled. Cut into bars. Cover; store leftover bars in refrigerator.

CHOCOLATE CRUST: Stir together 2 cups vanilla wafer crumbs (about 60 wafers, crushed), ⅓ cup HERSHEY'S Cocoa and ½ cup powdered sugar. Stir in ½ cup (1 stick) melted butter or margarine until well blended. Press mixture firmly onto bottom of ungreased 13×9×2-inch baking pan.

HERSHEY'S

Cakes
& Cheesecakes

Brickle Bundt Cake

Makes 12 to 14 servings

1⅓ cups (8-ounce package) HEATH BITS 'O BRICKLE Toffee
  Bits, divided
1¼ cups granulated sugar, divided
¼ cup chopped walnuts
1 teaspoon ground cinnamon
½ cup (1 stick) butter, softened
2 eggs
1¼ teaspoons vanilla extract, divided
2 cups all-purpose flour
1½ teaspoons baking powder
1 teaspoon baking soda
¼ teaspoon salt
1 container (8 ounces) dairy sour cream
¼ cup (½ stick) butter, melted
1 cup powdered sugar
1 to 3 tablespoons milk, divided

1. Heat oven to 325°F. Grease and flour 12-cup fluted tube pan
or 10-inch tube pan. Set aside ¼ cup toffee bits for topping.
Combine remaining toffee bits, ¼ cup granulated sugar, walnuts
and cinnamon; set aside.

2. Beat remaining 1 cup granulated sugar and ½ cup butter in large bowl until fluffy. Add eggs and 1 teaspoon vanilla; beat well. Stir together flour, baking powder, baking soda and salt; gradually add to butter mixture alternately with sour cream, beating until blended. Beat 3 minutes. Spoon one-third of the batter into prepared pan. Sprinkle with half of toffee mixture. Spoon half of remaining batter into pan. Top with remaining toffee mixture. Spoon remaining batter into pan. Pour melted butter over batter.

3. Bake 45 to 50 minutes or until wooden pick inserted near center comes out clean. Cool 10 minutes; remove from pan to wire rack. Cool completely.

4. Stir together powdered sugar, 1 tablespoon milk and remaining ¼ teaspoon vanilla. Stir in additional milk, 1 teaspoon at a time, until desired consistency; drizzle over cake. Sprinkle with reserved ¼ cup toffee bits.

HERSHEY'S

HERSHEY'S HUGS and KISSES
Candies Chocolate Cake

Makes 12 to 15 servings

¾   **cup (1½ sticks) butter or margarine, softened**
1¾ **cups sugar**
2   **eggs**
1   **teaspoon vanilla extract**
2   **cups all-purpose flour**
¾   **cup HERSHEY'S Cocoa or HERSHEY'S SPECIAL DARK Cocoa**
1¼ **teaspoons baking soda**
½   **teaspoon salt**
1⅓ **cups water**
   COCOA FUDGE FROSTING (recipe follows)
   HERSHEY'S HUGSBRAND **Candies or HERSHEY'S KISSES**BRAND **Milk Chocolates**

1. Heat oven to 350°F. Grease and flour 13×9×2-inch baking pan.

2. Beat butter and sugar in large bowl until fluffy. Add eggs and vanilla; beat 1 minute on medium speed of mixer. Stir together flour, cocoa, baking soda and salt; add alternately with water to butter mixture, beating until well blended. Pour batter into prepared pan.

3. Bake 40 to 45 minutes or until wooden pick inserted in center comes out clean. Cool 10 minutes; remove from pan to wire rack. Cool completely. Frost with COCOA FUDGE FROSTING. Remove wrappers from candies; garnish cake as desired with candies.

HERSHEY'S

Cocoa Fudge Frosting

Makes about 2½ cups frosting

- ½ **cup (1 stick) butter or margarine**
- ½ **cup HERSHEY'S Cocoa or HERSHEY'S SPECIAL DARK Cocoa**
- 3⅔ **cups (1 pound) powdered sugar**
- ⅓ **cup milk, heated**
- 1 **teaspoon vanilla extract**

Melt butter in small saucepan over low heat; stir in cocoa. Cook, stirring constantly, until mixture thickens slightly. Remove from heat; pour into small mixer bowl. Add powdered sugar alternately with warm milk, beating to spreading consistency. Stir in vanilla. Spread frosting while warm.

HERSHEY'S

Dandy Cake

Makes 20 to 24 servings

1 **cup water**
1 **cup (2 sticks) butter or margarine**
⅓ **cup HERSHEY'S Cocoa**
2 **cups all-purpose flour**
2 **cups sugar**
1 **teaspoon baking soda**
½ **teaspoon salt**
3 **eggs**
¾ **cup dairy sour cream**
¾ **cup REESE'S Creamy Peanut Butter**
CHOCOLATE TOPPING (recipe follows)

1. Heat oven to 350°F. Grease and flour 15½×10½×1-inch jelly-roll pan.

2. Combine water, butter and cocoa in small saucepan. Cook over medium heat, stirring occasionally, until mixture boils; boil and stir 1 minute. Remove from heat; set aside.

3. Stir together flour, sugar, baking soda and salt in large bowl. Add eggs and sour cream; beat until well blended. Add cocoa mixture; beat just until blended (batter will be thin). Pour into prepared pan.

4. Bake 25 to 30 minutes or until wooden pick inserted in center comes out clean. Do not remove cake from pan. Spread peanut butter over warm cake. Cool completely in pan on wire rack. Prepare CHOCOLATE TOPPING; carefully spread over top, covering peanut butter. Allow topping to set; cut into squares.

HERSHEY'S

CHOCOLATE TOPPING: Place 2 cups (12-ounce package) HERSHEY'S SPECIAL DARK Chocolate Chips or HERSHEY'S Semi-Sweet Chocolate Chips and 2 tablespoons shortening (do not use butter, margarine, spread or oil) in small microwave-safe bowl. Microwave at MEDIUM (50%) 1½ minutes; stir. If necessary, microwave at MEDIUM an additional 15 seconds at a time, stirring after each heating, just until chips are melted when stirred.

HERSHEY'S

Chocolate & Peanut Butter Fudge Cheesecake

Makes 10 to 12 servings

1½ cups vanilla wafer crumbs (about 45 wafers, crushed)
½ cup powdered sugar
¼ cup HERSHEY'S Cocoa
⅓ cup butter or margarine, melted
3 packages (8 ounces each) cream cheese, softened
¾ cup granulated sugar
3 eggs
⅓ cup dairy sour cream
3 tablespoons all-purpose flour
1 teaspoon vanilla extract
¼ teaspoon salt
1 cup HERSHEY'S SPECIAL DARK Chocolate Chips or HERSHEY'S Semi-Sweet Chocolate Chips, melted
1 cup REESE'S Peanut Butter Chips, melted
HERSHEY'S Fudge Topping (optional)
Sweetened whipped cream (optional)

1. Heat oven to 350°F. Combine vanilla wafer crumbs, powdered sugar, cocoa and melted butter in medium bowl. Press onto bottom and 1 inch up side of 9-inch springform pan. Bake 8 minutes; cool.

2. Beat cream cheese and granulated sugar in large bowl until smooth. Add eggs, sour cream, flour, vanilla and salt; beat until well blended.

3. Place half of batter in separate bowl. Stir melted chocolate into one bowl of cream cheese mixture and melted peanut butter chips into the other. Spread chocolate mixture in prepared crust. Gently spread peanut butter mixture over chocolate mixture. Do not stir.

HERSHEY'S

4. Bake 50 to 55 minutes or until center is almost set. (For less cracking of cheesecake surface, bake in water bath.) Remove from oven to wire rack. With knife, loosen cake from side of pan. Cool completely; remove side of pan. Cover; refrigerate.

5. To serve, drizzle each slice with fudge topping and top with whipped cream, if desired. Cover; refrigerate leftover cheesecake.

HERSHEY'S

Macadamia
Nuts

White Chip and Macadamia Toffee Crunch

Makes 1 pound candy

- 1 cup HERSHEY'S Premier White Chips
- ½ cup MAUNA LOA Macadamia Nut Baking Pieces
- ¾ cup (1½ sticks) butter
- ¾ cup sugar
- 3 tablespoons light corn syrup

1. Line 8- or 9-inch square or round pan with foil, extending foil over edges of pan; butter foil. Stir together white chips and nuts. Reserve 2 tablespoons white chip and nut mixture; sprinkle remaining chip mixture over bottom of prepared pan.

2. Combine butter, sugar and corn syrup in heavy medium saucepan; cook over low heat, stirring constantly, until butter is melted and sugar is dissolved. Increase heat to medium; cook, stirring constantly, until mixture boils. Cook and stir until mixture turns a medium caramel color (about 15 minutes).

3. Immediately pour mixture over chip and nut mixture in pan, spreading evenly. Sprinkle reserved chip mixture over surface. Cool. Refrigerate until chips are firm. Remove from pan; peel off foil. Break into pieces. Store tightly covered in cool, dry place.

SPECIAL DARK AND MACADAMIA TOFFEE CRUNCH: Substitute 1 cup HERSHEY'S SPECIAL DARK Chocolate Chips for HERSHEY'S Premier White Chips.

HERSHEY'S

White Chip and Macadamia Nut Coffee Cake

Makes 12 to 16 servings

CRUMB TOPPING (recipe follows)
- 6 tablespoons butter or margarine, softened
- ¾ cup granulated sugar
- ¾ cup packed light brown sugar
- 2 cups all-purpose flour
- 2 teaspoons baking powder
- ½ teaspoon ground cinnamon
- 1¼ cups milk
- 1 egg
- 1 teaspoon vanilla extract
- WHITE DRIZZLE (recipe follows)

1. Heat oven to 350°F. Grease and flour 13×9×2-inch baking pan. Prepare CRUMB TOPPING; set aside.

2. Beat butter, granulated sugar and brown sugar until well blended. Stir together flour, baking powder and cinnamon; beat into butter mixture. Gradually add milk, egg and vanilla, beating until thoroughly blended. Pour ½ batter into prepared pan; top with ½ Crumb Topping. Gently spread remaining batter over topping. Sprinkle remaining topping over batter.

3. Bake 30 to 35 minutes or until wooden pick inserted into center comes out clean. Cool completely.

4. Prepare WHITE DRIZZLE; drizzle over cake.

HERSHEY'S

CRUMB TOPPING: Combine ⅔ cup packed light brown sugar, ½ cup all-purpose flour, 6 tablespoons firm butter or margarine, 1 cup HERSHEY'S Premier White Chips and ½ cup MAUNA LOA Macadamia Nut Baking Pieces in medium bowl. Mix until crumbly.

WHITE DRIZZLE: Beat together ¾ cup powdered sugar, 2 to 3 teaspoons milk, 1 teaspoon softened butter and ¼ teaspoon vanilla extract. If necessary, stir in additional milk ½ teaspoon at a time until desired consistency.

HERSHEY'S

HERSHEY'S SPECIAL DARK Chip
and Macadamia Nut Cookies

Makes 3½ dozen cookies

6	tablespoons butter, softened
⅓	cup butter-flavored shortening
½	cup packed light brown sugar
⅓	cup granulated sugar
1	egg
1½	teaspoons vanilla extract
1⅓	cups all-purpose flour
½	teaspoon baking soda
½	teaspoon salt
2	cups (12-ounce package) HERSHEY'S SPECIAL DARK Chocolate Chips
½	cup MAUNA LOA Macadamia Nut Baking Pieces

1. Heat oven to 350°F.

2. Beat butter and shortening in large bowl until well blended. Add brown sugar and granulated sugar; beat thoroughly. Add egg and vanilla, beating until well blended. Stir together flour, baking soda and salt; gradually beat into butter mixture. Stir in chocolate chips and nuts. Drop by rounded teaspoons onto ungreased cookie sheet.

3. Bake 10 to 12 minutes or until edges are lightly browned. Cool slightly; transfer to wire rack. Cool completely.

WHITE CHIPS AND MACADAMIA PIECES: Substitute 2 cups (12-ounce package) HERSHEY'S Premier White Chips for HERSHEY'S SPECIAL DARK Chips. Prepare as directed above.

CHOCOLATE COOKIE: Decrease flour to 1 cup; add ⅓ cup HERSHEY'S Cocoa or HERSHEY'S SPECIAL DARK Cocoa.

HERSHEY'S

Chocolate Macadamia Truffle Mousse Pie

Makes 6 to 8 servings

1   cup HERSHEY'S SPECIAL DARK Chocolate Chips, divided
½   cup MAUNA LOA Macadamia Nut Baking Pieces, divided
3   tablespoons plus 1 cup (½ pint) cold whipping cream
1   prepared chocolate crumb crust (6 ounces) or 1 baked
    (9-inch) pie crust, cooled
1   teaspoon unflavored gelatin
1   tablespoon cold water
2   tablespoons boiling water
½   cup sugar
¼   cup HERSHEY'S Cocoa
1   teaspoon vanilla extract
    Sweetened whipped cream or whipped topping

1. Set aside 2 tablespoons chocolate chips and 1 tablespoon nut pieces. Place remaining chips, nuts and 3 tablespoons whipping cream in medium microwave-safe bowl. Microwave at MEDIUM (50%) 1 minute; stir. If necessary, microwave at MEDIUM an additional 15 seconds at a time, stirring after each heating, until chips are melted when stirred. Spread mixture on bottom of prepared crust. Refrigerate while preparing next steps.

2. Sprinkle gelatin over cold water; let stand 1 minute to soften. Add boiling water; stir until gelatin is completely dissolved and mixture is clear. Cool slightly, about 5 minutes.

3. Meanwhile, stir together sugar and cocoa in small mixing bowl; add remaining 1 cup whipping cream and vanilla. Beat on high speed of electric mixer, scraping bottom of bowl occasionally, until stiff. Pour in gelatin mixture, beating until just well blended.

4. Carefully spread over chocolate layer in crust. Cover; refrigerate several hours or until firm. Garnish with whipped cream and reserved chips and nuts.

Cookies

Toffee Studded Snickerdoodles

Makes about 5 dozen cookies

- ½ cup (1 stick) butter or margarine, softened
- ½ cup shortening
- 1⅓ cups sugar, divided
- 2 eggs
- 2¾ cups all-purpose flour
- 2 teaspoons cream of tartar
- 1 teaspoon baking soda
- ¼ teaspoon salt
- 1⅓ cups (8-ounce package) HEATH BITS 'O BRICKLE Toffee Bits
- 2 teaspoons ground cinnamon

1. Heat oven to 400°F.

2. Beat butter, shortening and 1 cup sugar in large bowl until fluffy. Add eggs; beat thoroughly. Stir together flour, cream of tartar, baking soda and salt; gradually add to butter mixture, beating until well blended. Stir in toffee bits.

3. Stir together remaining ⅓ cup sugar and cinnamon. Shape dough into 1¼-inch balls; roll in sugar-cinnamon mixture. Place on ungreased cookie sheets.

4. Bake 9 to 11 minutes or until lightly browned around edges. Cool 1 minute; remove from cookie sheets to wire racks. Cool completely.

HERSHEY'S

HERSHEY'S MINI KISSES Milk Chocolate Peanut Butter Cookies

Makes 1½ dozen cookies

¼ cup (½ stick) butter or margarine, softened
¼ cup REESE'S Creamy Peanut Butter
¼ cup granulated sugar
¼ cup packed light brown sugar
1 egg
½ teaspoon vanilla extract
⅔ cup all-purpose flour
¼ teaspoon baking soda
⅛ teaspoon salt
1¾ cups (10-ounce package) HERSHEY'S MINI KISSES BRAND Milk Chocolates

1. Heat oven to 350°F. Lightly grease cookie sheet or line with parchment paper.

2. Beat butter and peanut butter in large bowl on medium speed of electric mixer until creamy. Gradually add granulated sugar and brown sugar, beating until well mixed. Add egg and vanilla; beat until light and fluffy. Stir together flour, baking soda and salt; add to butter mixture, beating until well blended. Stir in chocolates. Drop batter by rounded tablespoons onto prepared cookie sheet.

3. Bake 10 to 12 minutes or until lightly browned. Cool slightly; remove from cookie sheet to wire rack. Cool completely.

HERSHEY'S

Rich Dark Tiger Cookies

Makes about 4 dozen cookies

1½ **cups granulated sugar**
 ½ **cup vegetable oil**
 ½ **cup HERSHEY'S SPECIAL DARK Cocoa or HERSHEY'S Cocoa**
 3 **eggs**
1½ **teaspoons vanilla extract**
1¾ **cups all-purpose flour**
1½ **teaspoons baking powder**
 ½ **teaspoon salt**
   Powdered sugar
 48 **HERSHEY'S KISSES**BRAND **SPECIAL DARK Mildly Sweet Chocolates or HERSHEY'S KISSES**BRAND **Milk Chocolates, unwrapped (optional)**

1. Stir together granulated sugar and oil in large bowl; add cocoa, beating until well blended. Beat in eggs and vanilla. Stir together flour, baking powder and salt; gradually add to cocoa mixture, beating well.

2. Cover; refrigerate until dough is firm enough to handle, at least 6 hours.

3. Heat oven to 350°F. Grease cookie sheet or line with parchment paper. Shape dough into 1-inch balls (dough will still be sticky); roll in powdered sugar to coat. Place about 2 inches apart on prepared cookie sheet.

4. Bake 11 to 13 minutes or until almost no indentation remains when touched lightly and tops are cracked. Immediately press chocolate piece into center of each cookie, if desired. Cool slightly. Transfer to wire rack. Cool completely.

HERSHEY'S

Jolly Peanut Butter Gingerbread Cookies

Makes about 6 dozen cookies

1⅔	cups (10-ounce package) REESE'S Peanut Butter Chips
¾	cup (1½ sticks) butter or margarine, softened
1	cup packed light brown sugar
1	cup dark corn syrup
2	eggs
5	cups all-purpose flour
1	teaspoon baking soda
½	teaspoon ground cinnamon
¼	teaspoon ground ginger
¼	teaspoon salt

1. Place peanut butter chips in small microwave-safe bowl. Microwave at MEDIUM (50%) 1 minute; stir. If necessary, microwave at MEDIUM an additional 15 seconds at a time, stirring after each heating, until chips are melted when stirred. Beat melted peanut butter chips and butter in large bowl until well blended. Add brown sugar, corn syrup and eggs; beat until fluffy.

2. Stir together flour, baking soda, cinnamon, ginger and salt. Add half of flour mixture to butter mixture; beat on low speed of mixer until smooth. With wooden spoon, stir in remaining flour mixture until well blended. Divide into thirds; wrap each in plastic wrap. Refrigerate at least 1 hour or until dough is firm enough to roll.

3. Heat oven to 325°F. On lightly floured surface, roll 1 dough portion at a time to ⅛-inch thickness; cut into holiday shapes with floured cookie cutters. Place on ungreased cookie sheet.

4. Bake 10 to 12 minutes or until set and lightly browned. Cool slightly; remove from cookie sheet to wire rack. Cool completely. Frost and decorate as desired.

HERSHEY'S

Pies
& Desserts

Easy Chocolate Cheesepie

Makes 6 to 8 servings

- **4** sections (½ ounce each) HERSHEY'S Unsweetened Chocolate Baking Bar, broken into pieces
- **¼** cup (½ stick) butter or margarine, softened
- **¾** cup sugar
- **1** package (3 ounces) cream cheese, softened
- **1** teaspoon milk
- **2** cups frozen whipped topping, thawed
- **1** packaged crumb crust (6 ounces)
  Additional whipped topping (optional)

1. Place chocolate in small microwave-safe bowl. Microwave at MEDIUM (50%) 1 to 1½ minutes or until chocolate is melted and smooth when stirred.

2. Beat butter, sugar, cream cheese and milk in medium bowl until well blended and smooth; fold in melted chocolate.

3. Fold in 2 cups whipped topping; spoon into crust. Cover; refrigerate until firm, about 3 hours. Garnish with additional whipped topping, if desired.

HERSHEY'S

Chocolate Cups with Lemon Cream

Makes about 6 filled cups

½ **cup sugar**
¼ **cup plus 2 tablespoons all-purpose flour**
2 **tablespoons HERSHEY'S Cocoa**
2 **egg whites**
¼ **cup (½ stick) butter or margarine, melted**
   CHOCOLATE COATING (recipe follows)
   LEMON CREAM (recipe follows)
   Freshly shredded lemon peel (optional)

1. Heat oven to 400°F. Grease and flour cookie sheet.

2. Stir together sugar, flour and cocoa in small bowl. Add egg whites and butter; beat until smooth. Drop teaspoonfuls of mixture onto prepared baking sheet; with back of spoon, spread thinly into 5-inch circles.

3. Bake 6 to 7 minutes or until set. Immediately remove from cookie sheet; place, top side down, over bottom of inverted juice glasses. Mold to form wavy edges. (If chocolate cracks, gently press together with fingers.) Let stand about 30 minutes or until hard and completely cool.

4. Prepare CHOCOLATE COATING. With small brush, coat inside of cups with prepared coating. Refrigerate 20 minutes or until coating is set.

5. Meanwhile, prepare LEMON CREAM; spoon scant ½ cup LEMON CREAM into each cup. Garnish with shredded lemon peel, if desired. Cover; refrigerate leftover desserts.

Chocolate Coating

¾ cup HERSHEY'S SPECIAL DARK Chocolate Chips or HERSHEY'S Semi-Sweet Chocolate Chips

1 teaspoon shortening (do not use butter, margarine, spread or oil)

Place chocolate chips and shortening in small microwave-safe bowl. Microwave at MEDIUM (50%) 45 seconds; stir. If necessary, microwave at MEDIUM an additional 15 seconds at a time, stirring after each heating, just until chips are melted when stirred.

Lemon Cream

Makes about 2½ cups cream

1 package (4-serving size) instant lemon pudding & pie filling mix

1 cup milk

⅛ teaspoon lemon extract

1½ cups frozen non-dairy whipped topping, thawed

Combine pudding mix, milk and lemon extract in small bowl. Beat on low speed 2 minutes. Fold in whipped topping; refrigerate 30 minutes or until set.

HERSHEY'S

Baked Apple Slices with Peanut Butter Crumble

Makes 6 to 8 servings

4 **cups peeled and thinly sliced apples**
1 **cup sugar, divided**
1 **cup all-purpose flour, divided**
3 **tablespoons butter or margarine, divided**
1 **cup quick-cooking or old-fashioned rolled oats**
½ **teaspoon ground cinnamon**
1 **cup REESE'S Creamy Peanut Butter**
  Sweetened whipped cream or ice cream (optional)

1. Heat oven to 350°F. Grease 9-inch square baking pan.

2. Stir together apples, ¾ cup sugar and ¼ cup flour in large bowl. Spread in prepared pan; dot with 2 tablespoons butter. Combine oats, remaining ¾ cup flour, remaining ¼ cup sugar and cinnamon in medium bowl; set aside.

3. Place remaining 1 tablespoon butter and peanut butter in small microwave-safe bowl. Microwave at MEDIUM (50%) 30 seconds or until butter is melted; stir until smooth. Add to oat mixture; blend until crumbs are formed. Sprinkle crumb mixture over apples.

4. Bake 40 to 45 minutes or until apples are tender and edges are bubbly. Cool slightly. Serve warm or cool with whipped cream or ice cream, if desired.

Classic Boston Cream Pie

Makes 8 to 10 servings

⅓ **cup shortening**
1 **cup sugar**
2 **eggs**
1 **teaspoon vanilla extract**
1¼ **cups all-purpose flour**
1½ **teaspoons baking powder**
¼ **teaspoon salt**
¾ **cup milk**
   RICH FILLING (recipe follows)
   DARK COCOA GLAZE (recipe follows)

1. Heat oven to 350°F. Grease and flour 9-inch round baking pan.

2. Beat shortening, sugar, eggs and vanilla in large bowl until fluffy. Stir together flour, baking powder and salt; add alternately with milk to shortening mixture, beating well after each addition. Pour batter into prepared pan.

3. Bake 30 to 35 minutes or until wooden pick inserted in center comes out clean. Cool 10 minutes; remove from pan to wire rack. Cool completely.

HERSHEY'S

4. Prepare RICH FILLING. With long serrated knife, cut cake in half horizontally. Place one layer, cut side up, on serving plate; spread with prepared filling. Top with remaining layer, cut side down. Prepare DARK COCOA GLAZE; spread over cake, allowing glaze to run down sides. Refrigerate several hours or until cold. Garnish as desired. Refrigerate leftover dessert.

Rich Filling

Makes about 1⅓ cups filling

- ⅓ **cup sugar**
- 2 **tablespoons cornstarch**
- 1½ **cups milk**
- 2 **egg yolks, slightly beaten**
- 1 **tablespoon butter or margarine**
- 1 **teaspoon vanilla extract**

Stir together sugar and cornstarch in medium saucepan; gradually add milk and egg yolks, stirring until blended. Cook over medium heat, stirring constantly, until mixture comes to a boil. Boil 1 minute, stirring constantly. Remove from heat; stir in butter and vanilla. Cover; refrigerate several hours or until cold.

Dark Cocoa Glaze

Makes about ¾ cup glaze

- 3 **tablespoons water**
- 2 **tablespoons butter or margarine**
- 3 **tablespoons HERSHEY'S Cocoa**
- 1 **cup powdered sugar**
- ½ **teaspoon vanilla extract**

Heat water and butter in small saucepan over medium heat until mixture comes to a boil; remove from heat. Immediately stir in cocoa. Gradually add powdered sugar and vanilla, beating with whisk until smooth and of desired consistency; cool slightly.

HERSHEY'S

Chocolate & Peanut Butter Truffles

Makes about 3½ dozen candies

- ¾ cup (1½ sticks) butter (no substitutes)
- 1 cup REESE'S Peanut Butter Chips
- ½ cup HERSHEY'S Cocoa
- 1 can (14 ounces) sweetened condensed milk (not evaporated milk)
- 1 tablespoon vanilla extract
  HERSHEY'S Cocoa or finely chopped nuts or graham cracker crumbs

1. Melt butter and peanut butter chips in saucepan over very low heat. Add cocoa; stir until smooth. Add sweetened condensed milk; stir constantly until mixture is thick and glossy, about 4 minutes. Remove from heat; stir in vanilla.

2. Refrigerate 2 hours or until firm enough to handle. Shape into 1-inch balls; roll in cocoa, nuts or graham cracker crumbs. Refrigerate until firm, about 1 hour. Store, covered, in refrigerator.

HERSHEY'S
Timeless Treasures
CONTENTS

CAKES AND CHEESECAKES

Petit Mocha Cheesecakes

CRUMB CRUST
(recipe follows)

1 package (8 ounces) cream cheese, softened

1 cup sugar

2 eggs

1 teaspoon vanilla extract

⅓ cup HERSHEY'S Cocoa

2 tablespoons all-purpose flour

1 tablespoon powdered instant coffee

1 teaspoon hot water

CHOCOLATE GLAZE
(recipe follows, optional)

1. Heat oven to 375°F. Line small muffin cups (1¾ inches in diameter) with paper baking cups.

2. Prepare CRUMB CRUST. Place 1 slightly heaping teaspoon crumb mixture into each cup; press lightly. Beat cream cheese in large bowl until fluffy. Add sugar, eggs and vanilla; beat well. Add cocoa and flour; beat well. Dissolve coffee in water; add to chocolate mixture. Place about 1 tablespoon chocolate mixture into each cup.

3. Bake 15 to 18 minutes or until just set. Cool completely in pan on wire rack. Drizzle with CHOCOLATE GLAZE, if desired. Refrigerate until cold, about 2 hours. Cover; refrigerate leftover cheesecakes.

CRUMB CRUST: Stir together ½ cup graham cracker crumbs, 2 tablespoons powdered sugar and 2 tablespoons melted butter or margarine in small bowl until well combined.

CHOCOLATE GLAZE: Combine ¼ cup HERSHEY'S SPECIAL DARK Chocolate Chips or HERSHEY'S Semi-Sweet Chocolate Chips and 2 tablespoons whipping cream in small saucepan. Cook over very low heat, stirring constantly, until smooth. Use immediately.

Makes 42 cheesecakes

Chocolate Almond Cheesecake

ALMOND CRUMB
CRUST (recipe
follows)

3 packages (8 ounces
each) cream cheese,
softened

1¼ cups sugar

½ cup dairy sour cream

⅓ cup HERSHEY'S Cocoa

2 tablespoons all-purpose
flour

3 eggs

2 teaspoons almond
extract

1 teaspoon vanilla extract

ALMOND WHIPPED
CREAM (recipe
follows)

Sliced almonds
(optional)

1. Prepare ALMOND CRUMB CRUST.

2. Increase oven temperature to 425°F. Combine cream cheese, sugar, sour cream, cocoa and flour in large bowl; beat with electric mixer on medium speed until smooth. Add eggs, almond extract and vanilla; beat well. Pour into prepared crust.

3. Bake 10 minutes. Reduce oven temperature to 250°F; continue baking 55 minutes or until center appears set. Remove from oven to wire rack. With knife, loosen cake from side of pan. Cool completely; remove side of pan.

4. Refrigerate several hours before serving. Garnish with ALMOND WHIPPED CREAM and sliced almonds, if desired. Cover; refrigerate leftover cheesecake.

ALMOND CRUMB CRUST: Heat oven to 350°F. Stir together ¾ cup vanilla wafer crumbs (about 20 wafers, crushed), ½ cup ground blanched almonds and 3 tablespoons sugar in small bowl; stir in 3 tablespoons melted butter or margarine. Press mixture firmly onto bottom and ½ inch up side of 9-inch springform pan. Bake 8 to 10 minutes; cool slightly.

ALMOND WHIPPED CREAM: Combine ½ cup cold whipping cream, 2 tablespoons powdered sugar, ¼ teaspoon vanilla and ⅛ teaspoon almond extract in small bowl; beat until stiff. Makes 1 cup whipped cream.

Makes 10 to 12 servings

Orange-Glazed Cocoa Bundt Cake

¾ cup (1½ sticks) butter or margarine, softened

1⅔ cups sugar

2 eggs

1 teaspoon vanilla extract

¾ cup dairy sour cream

2 cups all-purpose flour

⅔ cup HERSHEY'S Cocoa

½ teaspoon salt

2 teaspoons baking soda

1 cup buttermilk or sour milk*

ORANGE GLAZE or VANILLA GLAZE (recipes follow)

To sour milk: Use 1 tablespoon white vinegar plus milk to equal 1 cup.

1. Heat oven to 350°F. Grease and flour 12-cup fluted tube pan.

2. Beat butter, sugar, eggs and vanilla in large bowl until light and fluffy; stir in sour cream. Stir together flour, cocoa and salt. Stir baking soda into buttermilk in medium bowl; add alternately with dry ingredients to butter mixture. Beat 2 minutes on medium speed. Pour batter into prepared pan.

3. Bake 50 minutes or until wooden pick inserted into center comes out clean. Cool in pan 10 minutes. Remove from pan to wire rack. Cool completely. Glaze with ORANGE GLAZE or VANILLA GLAZE; garnish as desired.

ORANGE GLAZE: Combine 2 cups powdered sugar, ¼ cup (½ stick) melted butter or margarine, 3 tablespoons orange juice, 1 teaspoon vanilla extract and ½ teaspoon freshly grated orange peel in medium bowl; beat until smooth. Makes 1 cup glaze.

VANILLA GLAZE: Substitute 3 tablespoons water for orange juice and omit orange peel.

Makes 12 to 14 servings

Rich HEATH Bits Cheesecake

VANILLA WAFER
CRUST (recipe
follows)
3 packages (8 ounces
each) cream cheese,
softened
1 cup sugar
3 eggs
1 container (8 ounces)
dairy sour cream
½ teaspoon vanilla extract
1⅓ cups (8-ounce package)
HEATH Milk Chocolate
Toffee Bits, divided

1. Prepare VANILLA WAFER CRUST. Heat oven to 350°F.

2. Beat cream cheese and sugar in large bowl on medium speed of mixer until well blended. Add eggs, one at a time, beating well after each addition. Add sour cream and vanilla; beat on low speed until blended.

3. Pour half of cheese mixture into crust. Reserve ¼ cup toffee bits for topping; sprinkle remaining toffee bits over cheese mixture in pan. Spoon in remaining cheese mixture.

4. Bake 1 hour or until filling is set. Cool 15 minutes. Sprinkle reserved toffee bits over top; with knife, loosen cake from side of pan. Cool completely; remove side of pan. Cover, refrigerate at least 4 hours before serving. Cover; refrigerate leftover cheesecake.

VANILLA WAFER CRUST: Combine 1¾ cups vanilla wafer crumbs (about 55 wafers, crushed) and 2 tablespoons sugar; stir in ¼ cup (½ stick) melted butter or margarine. Press onto bottom and 1 inch up side of 9-inch springform pan. Refrigerate about 30 minutes.

Makes 12 to 16 servings

COOKIES

Grandma's Favorite Sugarcakes

⅔ cup butter or margarine, softened

1½ cups packed light brown sugar

1 cup granulated sugar

2 eggs

2 teaspoons vanilla extract

4½ cups all-purpose flour

2 teaspoons baking soda

1 teaspoon baking powder

1 teaspoon salt

1 cup buttermilk or sour milk*

2 cups (12-ounce package) HERSHEY'S Mini Chips Semi-Sweet Chocolate

2 cups chopped walnuts or pecans

Vanilla frosting (optional)

Colored sugar or sprinkles (optional)

To sour milk: Use 1 tablespoon white vinegar plus milk to equal 1 cup.

1. Heat oven to 350°F. Grease cookie sheet.

2. Beat butter, brown sugar and granulated sugar until well blended in large mixing bowl. Add eggs and vanilla; beat until creamy. Stir together flour, baking soda, baking powder and salt; add alternately with buttermilk to butter mixture, beating well after each addition. Stir in chocolate chips and nuts. Drop by level ¼ cups or heaping tablespoons 2 inches apart onto prepared cookie sheet.

3. Bake 12 to 14 minutes or until golden brown. Cool slightly; remove to wire rack. Cool completely. Frost with favorite vanilla frosting; garnish with colored sugar, if desired.

Makes 3 dozen cookies

Classic MINI KISSES Cookie Mix (Cookie Mix in a Jar)

2¼ cups all-purpose flour

⅔ cup granulated sugar

1 teaspoon baking soda

½ teaspoon salt

1½ cups HERSHEY'S MINI KISSESʙʀᴀɴᴅ Milk Chocolates, divided

⅔ cup packed light brown sugar

BAKING INSTRUCTIONS (recipe follows)

1. Stir together flour, granulated sugar, baking soda and salt. Transfer mixture to clean 1-quart (4 cups) glass jar with lid; pack down into bottom of jar.

2. Layer with 1 cup chocolate pieces and brown sugar.* Top with remaining ½ cup chocolates; close jar. Attach card with BAKING INSTRUCTIONS.

To increase shelf life of mix, wrap brown sugar in plastic wrap and press into place.

Tip: *For best results, use cookie mix within 4 weeks of assembly.*

Makes 1 jar mix

Classic MINI KISSES Cookies

1 jar Classic MINI KISSESʙʀᴀɴᴅ Cookie Mix

1 cup (2 sticks) butter, softened and cut into pieces

1 teaspoon vanilla extract

2 eggs, lightly beaten

BAKING INSTRUCTIONS

1. Heat oven to 375°F.

2. Spoon contents of jar into large bowl; stir to break up any lumps. Add butter and vanilla extract; stir until crumbly mixture forms. Add eggs; stir to form smooth, very stiff dough. Drop by heaping teaspoons onto ungreased cookie sheet.

3. Bake 8 to 10 minutes or until lightly browned. Cool slightly; remove from cookie sheet to wire rack. Cool completely.

Makes 36 cookies

Chocolate-Cherry Slice 'n' Bake Cookies

¾ cup (1½ sticks) butter or margarine, softened

1 cup sugar

1 egg

1½ teaspoons vanilla extract

2¼ cups all-purpose flour

2 teaspoons baking powder

½ teaspoon salt

¼ cup finely chopped maraschino cherries

½ teaspoon almond extract

Red food color

⅓ cup HERSHEY'S Cocoa

¼ teaspoon baking soda

4 teaspoons water

COCOA ALMOND GLAZE (recipe follows, optional)

1. Beat butter, sugar, egg and vanilla in large bowl until fluffy. Stir together flour, baking powder and salt; gradually add to butter mixture, beating until mixture forms a smooth dough. Remove 1¼ cups dough to medium bowl; blend in cherries, almond extract and about 6 drops food color.

2. Stir together cocoa and baking soda. Add with water to remaining dough; blend until smooth. Divide chocolate dough in half; roll each half between two sheets of wax paper, forming 12×4½-inch rectangle. Remove top sheet of wax paper. Divide cherry mixture in half; with floured hands, shape each half into 12-inch roll. Place one roll in center of each rectangle; wrap chocolate dough around roll, forming one large roll. Wrap in plastic wrap. Refrigerate about 6 hours or until firm.

3. Heat oven to 350°F.

4. Cut rolls into ¼-inch-thick slices; place on ungreased cookie sheet. Bake 7 minutes or until set. Cool 1 minute; remove from cookie sheet to wire rack. Cool completely. Decorate cookies with COCOA ALMOND GLAZE, if desired.

Makes about 7½ dozen cookies

Cocoa Almond Glaze

2 tablespoons butter or margarine

2 tablespoons HERSHEY'S Cocoa

2 tablespoons water

1 cup powdered sugar

⅛ teaspoon almond extract

Melt butter in small saucepan over low heat. Add cocoa and water; stir constantly until mixture thickens. Do not boil. Remove from heat. Add powered sugar and almond extract, beating until smooth and of desired consistency. Add additional water, ½ teaspoon at a time, if needed.

Makes about ½ cup glaze

HERSHEY'S

PIES AND DESSERTS

Creamy Milk Chocolate Pudding Pie

⅔ cup sugar

6 tablespoons cornstarch

2 tablespoons HERSHEY'S Cocoa

½ teaspoon salt

3 cups milk

4 egg yolks

2 tablespoons butter or margarine, softened

1 tablespoon vanilla extract

5 HERSHEY'S Milk Chocolate bars (1.55 ounces each), broken into pieces

1 packaged chocolate crumb crust (6 ounces)

Sweetened whipped cream or whipped topping

Additional HERSHEY'S Milk Chocolate Bar (1.55 ounces), cut into sections along score lines (optional)

1. Stir together sugar, cornstarch, cocoa and salt in 2-quart saucepan. Combine milk and egg yolks in bowl or container with pouring spout. Gradually blend milk mixture into sugar mixture.

2. Cook over medium heat, stirring constantly, until mixture comes to a boil. Boil and stir 1 minute. Remove from heat; stir in butter and vanilla. Add remaining chocolate bars; stir until bars are melted and mixture is well blended. Pour into crumb crust; press plastic wrap onto filling. Cool. Refrigerate several hours or until chilled and firm. Remove plastic wrap. Garnish with whipped cream and reserved small chocolate bars. Cover; refrigerate leftovers.

Makes 6 to 8 servings

Easy Chip and Nut Gift Bread

2 cups all-purpose flour

1 cup granulated sugar

1 teaspoon baking powder

1 teaspoon salt

½ teaspoon baking soda

1 cup applesauce

½ cup shortening

2 eggs

1 cup HERSHEY'S Cinnamon Chips, HERSHEY'S SPECIAL DARK Chocolate Chips or HERSHEY'S Semi-Sweet Chocolate Chips

½ cup chopped walnuts

Powdered sugar (optional)

1. Heat oven to 350°F. Grease three 5¾×3¼×2-inch mini loaf pans.

2. Combine flour, granulated sugar, baking powder, salt, baking soda, applesauce, shortening and eggs in large bowl. Beat on medium speed of mixer until well blended. Stir in cinnamon chips and walnuts. Divide batter evenly into prepared pans.

3. Bake 45 minutes or until wooden pick inserted in center comes out clean. Cool 10 minutes; remove from pans to wire rack. Cool completely. Sprinkle with powdered sugar, if desired.

Makes 3 small loaves

Macadamia Nut Fudge

1½ cups sugar

1 jar (7 ounces) marshmallow crème

1 can (5 ounces) evaporated milk (about ⅔ cup)

¼ cup (½ stick) butter or margarine

2 cups (12-ounce package) HERSHEY'S SPECIAL DARK Chocolate Chips

1 cup MAUNA LOA Macadamia Nut Baking Pieces

½ teaspoon vanilla extract

1. Line 8- or 9-inch square pan with foil, extending foil over edges of pan.

2. Combine sugar, marshmallow crème, evaporated milk and butter in heavy medium saucepan. Cook over medium heat, stirring constantly, to a full boil. Boil, stirring constantly, 5 minutes.

3. Remove from heat; add chocolate chips. Stir just until chips are melted. Stir in nuts and vanilla; pour into prepared pan.

4. Refrigerate 1 hour or until firm. Lift fudge out of pan using foil; place on cutting board. Cut into squares. Store tightly covered in a cool, dry place.

Note: *For best results, do not double this recipe.*

Makes 2 pounds fudge

Mocha Brownie Nut Torte

1 cup (2 sticks) butter

1 package (4 ounces) HERSHEY'S Unsweetened Chocolate Baking Bar, broken into pieces

4 eggs

1 teaspoon vanilla extract

2 cups granulated sugar

1 cup all-purpose flour

1 cup finely chopped pecans

1 package (8 ounces) cream cheese, softened

1 cup powdered sugar

½ cup chilled whipping cream

2 to 3 teaspoons powdered instant coffee

CHOCOLATE GLAZE (recipe follows)

1. Heat oven to 350°F. Line bottom and sides of 9-inch round cake pan with foil, extending foil beyond sides. Grease foil.

2. Place butter and chocolate in medium microwave-safe bowl. Microwave at MEDIUM (50%) 1 minute; stir. If necessary, microwave an additional 15 seconds at a time, stirring after each heating, until chocolate is melted when stirred. Cool 5 minutes.

3. Beat eggs and vanilla in large bowl until foamy. Gradually beat in granulated sugar. Blend in chocolate mixture; fold in flour and pecans. Spread mixture in prepared pan. Bake 40 to 45 minutes or until wooden pick inserted in center comes out clean. Cool completely in pan on wire rack.

4. Use foil to lift brownie from pan; remove foil. Place brownie layer on serving plate. Beat cream cheese and powdered sugar in medium bowl until well blended. Beat whipping cream and instant coffee until stiff; gradually fold into cream cheese mixture, blending well. Spread over brownie layer. Cover; refrigerate until serving time.

5. Just before serving, prepare CHOCOLATE GLAZE. Drizzle generous tablespoon glaze over top and down sides of each serving.

Makes 10 to 12 servings

CHOCOLATE GLAZE: Place 6 ounces (1½ 4-ounce packages) HERSHEY'S Semi-Sweet Chocolate Baking Bar and ½ cup whipping cream in small microwave-safe bowl. Microwave at MEDIUM (50%) 30 to 45 seconds or until chocolate is melted and mixture is smooth when stirred. Cool slightly.

Makes 1 cup glaze

Chocolate Harvest Nut Pie

½ cup packed light brown sugar

⅓ cup HERSHEY'S Cocoa

¼ teaspoon salt

1 cup light corn syrup

3 eggs

3 tablespoons butter or margarine, melted

1½ teaspoons vanilla extract

½ cup coarsely chopped pecans

½ cup coarsely chopped walnuts

¼ cup slivered almonds

1 unbaked (9-inch) pie crust

Whipped topping (optional)

1. Heat oven to 350°F. Stir together brown sugar, cocoa and salt. Add corn syrup, eggs, butter and vanilla; stir until well blended. Stir in pecans, walnuts and almonds. Pour into unbaked pie crust. To prevent overbrowning of crust, cover edge of pie with foil.

2. Bake 30 minutes. Remove foil. Bake additional 25 to 30 minutes or until puffed across top. Remove from oven to wire rack. Cool completely.

3. Garnish with whipped topping and additional nuts, if desired. Cover; store leftover pie in refrigerator.

Makes 8 servings

Spicy Cocoa Glazed Pecans

¼ cup plus 2 tablespoons sugar, divided
1 cup warm water
1½ cups pecan halves or pieces
1 tablespoon HERSHEY'S Cocoa
3 to 4 teaspoons chili powder
⅛ to ¼ teaspoon cayenne pepper

1. Heat oven to 350°F. Lightly spray shallow baking pan with vegetable cooking spray.

2. Stir together ¼ cup sugar and warm water, stirring until sugar dissolves. Add pecans; let soak 10 minutes. Drain water and discard.

3. Stir together remaining 2 tablespoons sugar, cocoa, chili powder and cayenne pepper in medium bowl. Add pecans; toss until all cocoa mixture coats pecans. Spread coated pecans on prepared pan.

4. Bake 10 to 15 minutes or until pecans start to glisten and appear dry. Stir occasionally while baking. Cool completely. Store in cool, dry place. Serve as a snack with beverages or sprinkle in salads.

Makes 1½ cups coated pecans

Chicken Satay Skewers

6 garlic cloves, chopped

4 teaspoons dried coriander

4 teaspoons light brown sugar

2 teaspoons salt

1½ teaspoons HERSHEY'S Cocoa

1 teaspoon ground black pepper

½ cup soy sauce

6 tablespoons vegetable oil

2 tablespoons lime juice

4 teaspoons fresh chopped ginger

2½ pounds boneless, skinless chicken breasts

PEANUT DIPPING SAUCE (recipe follows)

¼ cup fresh cilantro, chopped (optional)

1. Combine garlic, coriander, brown sugar, salt, cocoa and pepper in large bowl. Stir in soy sauce, oil, lime juice and ginger.

2. Cut chicken into 1½- to 2-inch cubes. Add to soy sauce mixture, stirring to coat chicken pieces. Cover; marinate in refrigerator for at least 2 hours.

3. Meanwhile, prepare PEANUT DIPPING SAUCE. Thread chicken pieces onto skewers. Grill or broil, basting with marinade. Discard leftover marinade. Garnish with chopped cilantro, if desired. Serve with PEANUT DIPPING SAUCE. Refrigerate leftovers.

Makes 15 to 20 appetizers or 4 to 6 entrée servings

Peanut Dipping Sauce

½ cup peanut oil

1 cup REESE'S Creamy
  Peanut Butter

¼ cup lime juice

¼ cup soy sauce

3 tablespoons honey

2 garlic cloves, minced

1 teaspoon cayenne
  pepper

½ teaspoon hot pepper
  sauce

Gradually whisk peanut oil into peanut butter in
medium bowl. Blend in lime juice, soy sauce,
honey, garlic, cayenne pepper and hot pepper
sauce. Adjust flavors to taste for a sweet/hot flavor.

Makes 2¼ cups

Ranch-Style Shrimp and Bacon Appetizers

RANCH-STYLE
BARBECUE SAUCE
(recipe follows)

30 large peeled, deveined shrimp

½ pound thick-cut bacon

10 wooden skewers*

To prevent wooden skewers from burning while grilling or broiling, soak in water about 10 minutes before using.

1. Prepare RANCH-STYLE BARBECUE SAUCE.

2. Wrap each shrimp with ½ bacon strip. Thread 3 wrapped shrimp onto each wooden skewer.

3. Grill or broil shrimp skewers until bacon is cooked and shrimp is no longer translucent, but has turned pink. Baste with RANCH-STYLE BARBECUE SAUCE. Return to heat to warm sauce. Serve with additional RANCH-STYLE BARBECUE SAUCE, if desired.

Makes 10 shrimp skewers

Ranch-Style Barbecue Sauce

¼ cup vegetable or olive oil

½ cup minced onion

2 garlic cloves, minced

2 tablespoons lemon juice

1 tablespoon ground black pepper

1 teaspoon dry mustard

1 teaspoon paprika

½ teaspoon salt

½ teaspoon hot pepper sauce

1½ cups ketchup

1 cup HEATH BITS 'O BRICKLE Toffee Bits

¼ cup cider vinegar

3 tablespoons sugar

1½ tablespoons HERSHEY'S Cocoa

1. Heat oil in large saucepan over medium heat; add onion and garlic. Cook until tender. Stir in lemon juice, black pepper, mustard, paprika, salt and hot pepper sauce. Simmer for 5 minutes; reduce heat.

2. Stir in ketchup, toffee bits, vinegar, sugar and cocoa. Simmer 15 minutes. Refrigerate leftovers.

Makes 3 cups

Smokey Chili with Pasta

2 cups (about 6 ounces) rotelle or rotini pasta, uncooked

1 pound ground beef

1 cup chopped onion

2 cans (about 15 ounces each) red kidney beans

2 cans (10¾ ounces each) condensed tomato soup

2 tablespoons HERSHEY'S Cocoa

2¼ teaspoons chili powder

¾ teaspoon ground black pepper

½ teaspoon salt

Grated Parmesan cheese (optional)

1. Cook pasta according to package directions; drain.

2. Meanwhile, cook ground beef and onion until meat is thoroughly done and onion is tender. If necessary, drain fat.

3. Stir in undrained kidney beans, soup, cocoa, chili powder, pepper and salt. Heat to boiling; reduce heat. Stir in hot pasta; heat thoroughly. Serve with Parmesan cheese, if desired.

Makes 8 servings

BROWNIES AND BARS

Perfectly Peppermint Brownies

¾ cup HERSHEY'S Cocoa
½ teaspoon baking soda
⅔ cup butter or margarine, melted and divided
½ cup boiling water
2 cups sugar
2 eggs
1⅓ cups all-purpose flour
1 teaspoon vanilla extract
¼ teaspoon salt
16 to 17 small (1½-inch) YORK Peppermint Patties, unwrapped and coarsely chopped

1. Heat oven to 350°F. Grease 13×9×2-inch baking pan.

2. Stir together cocoa and baking soda in large bowl; stir in ⅓ cup butter. Add boiling water; stir until mixture thickens. Stir in sugar, eggs and remaining ⅓ cup butter; stir until smooth. Add flour, vanilla and salt; blend completely. Stir in peppermint pattie pieces. Spread in prepared pan.

3. Bake 35 to 40 minutes or until brownies begin to pull away from sides of pan. Cool completely in pan on wire rack. Cut into bars.

Makes about 3 dozen brownies

Simply Special Brownies

½ cup (1 stick) butter or margarine

1 package (4 ounces) HERSHEY'S Semi-Sweet Chocolate Baking Bar, broken into pieces

2 eggs

1 teaspoon vanilla extract

¾ teaspoon powdered instant coffee

⅔ cup sugar

½ cup all-purpose flour

¼ teaspoon baking soda

¼ teaspoon salt

½ cup coarsely chopped nuts (optional)

1. Heat oven to 350°F. Grease 9-inch square baking pan.

2. Place butter and chocolate in medium microwave-safe bowl. Microwave at MEDIUM (50%) 1 minute; stir. If necessary, microwave an additional 15 seconds at a time, stirring after each heating, until chocolate is melted and mixture is smooth when stirred. Add eggs, vanilla and instant coffee, stirring until well blended. Stir in sugar, flour, baking soda and salt; blend completely. Stir in nuts, if desired. Spread batter in prepared pan.

3. Bake 25 to 30 minutes or until wooden pick inserted in center comes out almost clean. Cool completely in pan on wire rack. Cut into bars.

Makes 20 brownies

S'mores Sandwich Bar Cookies

½ cup (1 stick) butter or margarine, softened

¾ cup sugar

1 egg

1 teaspoon vanilla extract

1⅓ cups all-purpose flour

¾ cup graham cracker crumbs

1 teaspoon baking powder

¼ teaspoon salt

5 HERSHEY'S Milk Chocolate Bars (1.55 ounce each), broken in pieces

3 cups miniature marshmallows

1. Heat oven to 350°F. Grease 8-inch square baking pan.

2. Beat butter and sugar in large bowl until well blended. Add egg and vanilla; beat well. Stir together flour, graham cracker crumbs, baking powder and salt; add to butter mixture, beating until blended. Press half of dough into prepared pan. Bake 15 minutes.

3. Sprinkle chocolate bar sections, marshmallows and bits of remaining dough over baked layer. Bake 10 to 15 minutes or just until lightly browned. Cool completely in pan on wire rack. Cut into bars.

Makes 16 bars

Chocolate Almond Macaroon Bars

2 cups chocolate wafer cookie crumbs

6 tablespoons butter or margarine, melted

6 tablespoons powdered sugar

1 can (14 ounces) sweetened condensed milk (not evaporated milk)

3¾ cups MOUNDS Sweetened Coconut Flakes

1 cup sliced almonds, toasted* (optional)

1 cup HERSHEY'S SPECIAL DARK Chocolate Chips or HERSHEY'S Semi-Sweet Chocolate Chips

¼ cup whipping cream

½ cup HERSHEY'S Premier White Chips

To toast almonds: Heat oven to 350°F. Spread almonds evenly on shallow baking sheet. Bake 5 to 8 minutes or until lightly browned.

1. Heat oven to 350°F. Grease 13×9×2-inch baking pan.

2. Combine crumbs, melted butter and powdered sugar in large bowl. Firmly press crumb mixture on bottom of prepared pan. Stir together sweetened condensed milk, coconut and almonds in large bowl, mixing well. Carefully drop mixture by spoonfuls over crust; spread evenly.

3. Bake 20 to 25 minutes or until coconut edges just begin to brown. Cool.

4. Place chocolate chips and whipping cream in medium microwave-safe bowl. Microwave at MEDIUM (50%) 1 minute; stir. If necessary, microwave at MEDIUM an additional 15 seconds at a time, stirring after each heating, until chips are melted and mixture is smooth when stirred. Cool until slightly thickened; spread over cooled bars. Sprinkle top with white chips. Cover; refrigerate several hours or until thoroughly chilled. Cut into bars. Refrigerate leftovers.

Makes about 36 bars

Layered Cookie Bars

¾ cup (1½ sticks) butter
   or margarine

1¾ cups vanilla wafer
   crumbs (about
   50 wafers, crushed)

6 tablespoons
   HERSHEY'S Cocoa

¼ cup sugar

1 can (14 ounces)
   sweetened condensed
   milk (not evaporated
   milk)

1 cup HERSHEY'S
   SPECIAL DARK
   Chocolate Chips or
   HERSHEY'S Semi-
   Sweet Chocolate Chips

¾ cup HEATH BITS 'O
   BRICKLE Toffee Bits

1 cup chopped walnuts

1. Heat oven to 350°F. Melt butter in 13×9×2-inch baking pan in oven. Combine crumbs, cocoa and sugar; sprinkle over butter.

2. Pour sweetened condensed milk evenly on top of crumbs. Top with chocolate chips and toffee bits, then nuts; press down firmly.

3. Bake 25 to 30 minutes or until lightly browned. Cool completely in pan on wire rack. Chill, if desired. Cut into bars. Store covered at room temperature.

Makes about 36 bars

Double Chip Brownies

¾ cup HERSHEY'S Cocoa

½ teaspoon baking soda

⅔ cup butter or margarine, melted and divided

½ cup boiling water

2 cups sugar

2 eggs

1⅓ cups all-purpose flour

1 teaspoon vanilla extract

¼ teaspoon salt

1 cup HERSHEY'S Milk Chocolate Chips

1 cup REESE'S Peanut Butter Chips

1. Heat oven to 350°F. Grease 13×9×2-inch baking pan.

2. Stir together cocoa and baking soda in large bowl; stir in ⅓ cup melted butter. Add boiling water; stir until mixture thickens. Stir in sugar, eggs and remaining ⅓ cup melted butter; stir until smooth. Add flour, vanilla and salt; blend thoroughly. Stir in milk chocolate chips and peanut butter chips. Spread in prepared pan.

3. Bake 35 to 40 minutes or until brownies begin to pull away from sides of pan. Cool completely in pan on wire rack. Cut into squares.

Makes about 36 brownies

METRIC CONVERSION CHART

VOLUME MEASUREMENTS (dry)

⅛ teaspoon = 0.5 mL
¼ teaspoon = 1 mL
½ teaspoon = 2 mL
¾ teaspoon = 4 mL
1 teaspoon = 5 mL
1 tablespoon = 15 mL
2 tablespoons = 30 mL
¼ cup = 60 mL
⅓ cup = 75 mL
½ cup = 125 mL
⅔ cup = 150 mL
¾ cup = 175 mL
1 cup = 250 mL
2 cups = 1 pint = 500 mL
3 cups = 750 mL
4 cups = 1 quart = 1 L

VOLUME MEASUREMENTS (fluid)

1 fluid ounce (2 tablespoons) = 30 mL
4 fluid ounces (½ cup) = 125 mL
8 fluid ounces (1 cup) = 250 mL
12 fluid ounces (1½ cups) = 375 mL
16 fluid ounces (2 cups) = 500 mL

WEIGHTS (mass)

½ ounce = 15 g
1 ounce = 30 g
3 ounces = 90 g
4 ounces = 120 g
8 ounces = 225 g
10 ounces = 285 g
12 ounces = 360 g
16 ounces = 1 pound = 450 g

DIMENSIONS

$\frac{1}{16}$ inch = 2 mm
⅛ inch = 3 mm
¼ inch = 6 mm
½ inch = 1.5 cm
¾ inch = 2 cm
1 inch = 2.5 cm

OVEN TEMPERATURES

250°F = 120°C
275°F = 140°C
300°F = 150°C
325°F = 160°C
350°F = 180°C
375°F = 190°C
400°F = 200°C
425°F = 220°C
450°F = 230°C

BAKING PAN SIZES

Utensil	Size in Inches/Quarts	Metric Volume	Size in Centimeters
Baking or Cake Pan (square or rectangular)	8×8×2	2 L	20×20×5
	9×9×2	2.5 L	23×23×5
	12×8×2	3 L	30×20×5
	13×9×2	3.5 L	33×23×5
Loaf Pan	8×4×3	1.5 L	20×10×7
	9×5×3	2 L	23×13×7
Round Layer Cake Pan	8×1½	1.2 L	20×4
	9×1½	1.5 L	23×4
Pie Plate	8×1¼	750 mL	20×3
	9×1¼	1 L	23×3
Baking Dish or Casserole	1 quart	1 L	—
	1½ quarts	1.5 L	—
	2 quarts	2 L	—